EYEWITNESS
BIBLE LANDS

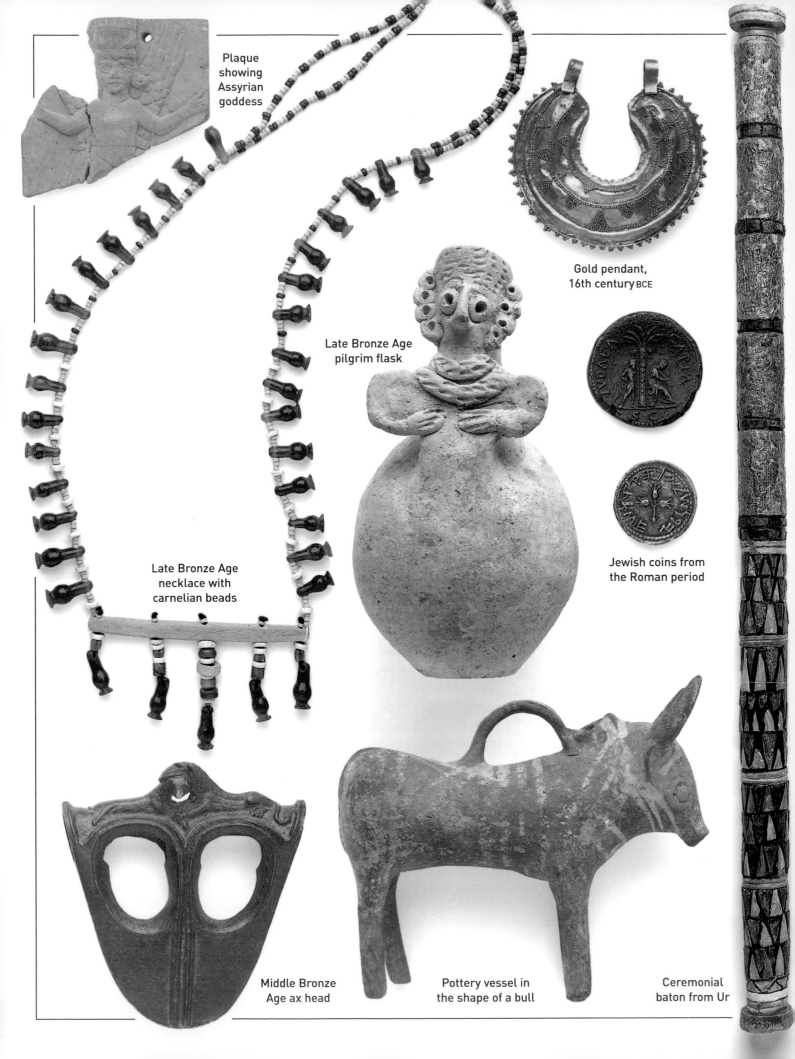

Plaque showing Assyrian goddess

Gold pendant, 16th century BCE

Late Bronze Age pilgrim flask

Jewish coins from the Roman period

Late Bronze Age necklace with carnelian beads

Middle Bronze Age ax head

Pottery vessel in the shape of a bull

Ceremonial baton from Ur

Gold earrings from
the Roman period

EYEWITNESS
BIBLE
LANDS

Written by
JONATHAN N. TUBB

Bronze
and gold
toggle
pins

Assyrian
lion carving

Ivory plaque
from Nimrud,
8th century BCE

Phoenician
glass
vessels

Ivory carved head,
13th century BCE

DK

Ivory duck's
head found
at Lachish

Bronze
lamp from
Roman period

Egyptian-style seal

Frieze
showing
Persian
palace guard

DK | Penguin Random House

Project editor Phil Wilkinson
Art editor Martin Atcherley
Senior editor Helen Parker
Senior art editor Julia Harris
Production Louise Barratt
Picture research Diana Morris
Special photography Alan Hills and Barbara Winter
of the British Museum, Karl Shone

RELAUNCH EDITION

DK UK
Consultant Philip Parker
Senior editor Chris Hawkes
Senior art editor Spencer Holbrook
US senior editor Margaret Parrish
Jacket editor Claire Gell
Jacket designer Natalie Godwin
Jacket design development manager
Sophia MTT
Producer, pre-production Gillian Reid
Producer Vivienne Yong
Managing editor Linda Esposito
Managing art editor Philip Letsu
Publisher Andrew Macintyre
Associate publishing director Liz Wheeler
Design director Stuart Jackman
Publishing director Jonathan Metcalf

DK INDIA
Senior editor Bharti Bedi
Editorial team Sheryl Sadana,
Antara Moitra
Design team Pooja Pipil, Nidhi Rastogi,
Nishesh Batnagar
Senior DTP designer Harish Aggarwal
DTP designer Pawan Kumar
Picture researcher Nishwan Rasool
Jacket designer Dhirendra Singh
Managing jackets editor Saloni Singh
Managing editor Kingshuk Ghoshal
Managing art editor Govind Mittal
Pre-production manager
Balwant Singh
Production manager
Pankaj Sharma

First American Edition, 1991
This edition published in the United States in 2016 by
DK Publishing, 345 Hudson Street, New York, New York 10014

Copyright © 1991, 2016 Dorling Kindersley Limited
DK, a Division of Penguin Random House LLC

16 17 18 19 20 10 9 8 7 6 5 4 3 2 1
001—287339—Jun/16

Published in Great Britain by Dorling Kindersley Limited.

A catalog record for this book is available from the Library of Congress.

ISBN: 978-1-4654-4010-5 (Paperback)
ISBN: 978-1-4654-4011-2 (ALB)

DK books are available at special discounts when purchased in bulk for sales
promotions, premiums, fund-raising, or educational use. For details, contact:
DK Publishing Special Markets, 345 Hudson Street, New York, New York 10014
SpecialSales@dk.com

Printed and bound in China

A WORLD OF IDEAS:
SEE ALL THERE IS TO KNOW

www.dk.com

Carved ivory
found at Nimrud

Persian
silver stag

Persian
silver bowl

Selection of
arrowheads

Contents

Ivory carving showing
winged sphinx

Lands of the Bible

The landscape of the Holy Land is made up of four different kinds of terrain. The coastal plain is dry in the south, with areas of marsh and lagoon in the north. The second zone is the hill country behind the coast where fertile west-facing slopes rise to form rocky ridges. The third zone, the Jordan Valley, has almost no rain. The highlands of Jordan and the plateau beyond make up the fourth zone.

Fishing boats on the Sea of Galilee

The Bible Lands

The Holy Land, also referred to at different times in its history as Palestine and Canaan, lies in the Levant (the eastern Mediterranean). This map shows some of the most important places mentioned in this book, together with the seas and lakes and the Jordan River.

Basilica of the Annunciation, Nazareth

MOUNT HERMON

• Tell Dan

Lake Huleh

• Hazor

• Capernaum

SEA OF GALILEE

PHOENICIA

PLAIN OF PHOENICIA

• Tyre

UPPER GALILEE

• Tiberias

LOWER GALILEE

GILEAD

Jordan River

• Tell es-Sa'idiyeh

• Acre

• Nazareth

• Beth Shan

MOUNT CARMEL

• Megiddo

SAMARIA

PLAIN OF SHARON

• Caesarea

• Samaria

• Tirzah

MEDITERRANEAN SEA

"Lot's wife"—a pillar of rock near the Dead Sea

By the Dead Sea, looking east to the hills of Moab

Ruins of Herod's palace, Masada

View of Temple Mount, Jerusalem

View of ancient part of Hebron city

PEREA

MOAB

EDOM

Tiwal esh-Sharqi

Jordan River

Qumran

Jericho

MOUNT
EPHRAIM

Ramathaim

JUDEA

Jerusalem

Bethlehem

Herodium

JUDEAN
HILLS

Hebron

Tel Gezer

DEAD
SEA

Masada

JUDEAN
DESERT

NEGEV

Ashdod

Lachish

PLAIN OF
PHILISTIA

Beer-sheba

Gaza

Early ancestors

Much of our knowledge of early life in the Holy Land comes from the site of Jericho, near the northern end of the Dead Sea. Here, Middle Stone Age (Mesolithic) hunters began to establish settlements from about 10,000 BCE. Over time, small farming villages sprang up, and people began to cultivate crops and domesticate animals. During the New Stone Age (or Neolithic period, about 8000–4500 BCE), tools and weapons were made from stone, flint, and obsidian (a type of volcanic glass). The people of the pre-pottery Neolithic period were skilled weavers, carpenters, and sculptors. Pottery was first made in about 7000 BCE. Copper-smelting developed about 1,000 years later, during the period known as the Chalcolithic.

Painted eyes

Face art
In the early Neolithic period, skulls were sometimes removed and used in ancestor worship. The facial features of the dead person were recreated in plaster, and hair was painted red or black. This example (above) was found in Jericho.

First city
In contrast to the simple villages of the early Neolithic period, Jericho grew into a city, with huge walls and at least one large stone tower (above).

Scrapers
Even after copper-working began, people still used tools made of flint. Scrapers such as these (right) were used to prepare animal skins for clothes.

Fan scraper

Scraper

Stony face
This carved limestone face mask dates to the pre-pottery Neolithic period.

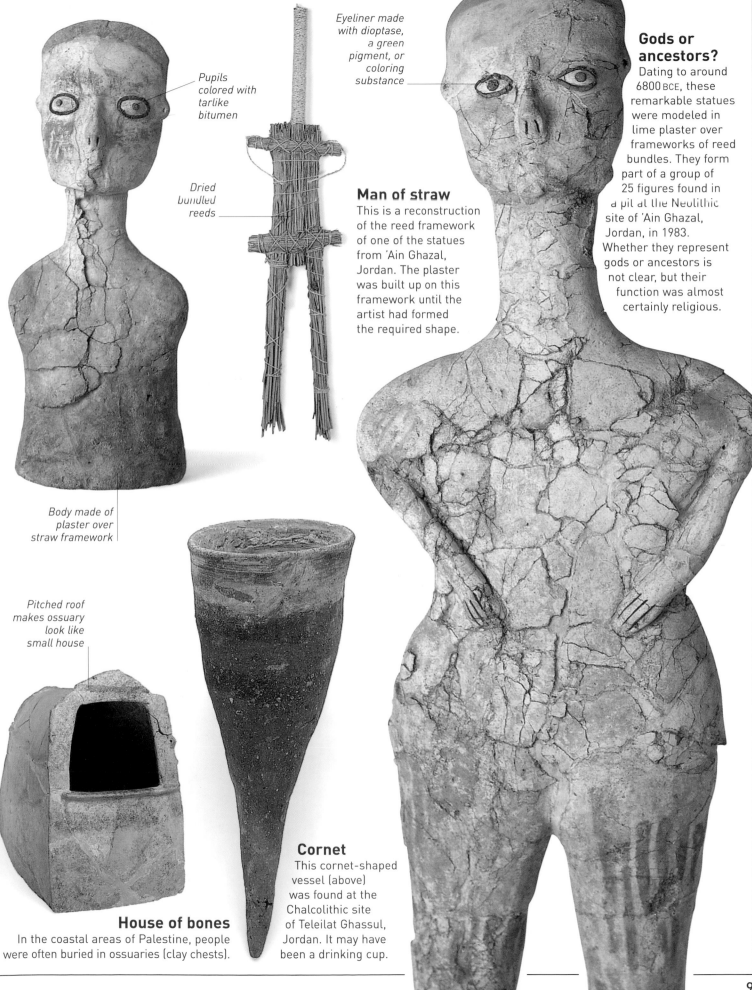

Pupils colored with tarlike bitumen

Body made of plaster over straw framework

Eyeliner made with dioptase, a green pigment, or coloring substance

Dried bundled reeds

Man of straw
This is a reconstruction of the reed framework of one of the statues from 'Ain Ghazal, Jordan. The plaster was built up on this framework until the artist had formed the required shape.

Gods or ancestors?
Dating to around 6800 BCE, these remarkable statues were modeled in lime plaster over frameworks of reed bundles. They form part of a group of 25 figures found in a pit at the Neolithic site of 'Ain Ghazal, Jordan, in 1983. Whether they represent gods or ancestors is not clear, but their function was almost certainly religious.

Pitched roof makes ossuary look like small house

House of bones
In the coastal areas of Palestine, people were often buried in ossuaries (clay chests).

Cornet
This cornet-shaped vessel (above) was found at the Chalcolithic site of Teleilat Ghassul, Jordan. It may have been a drinking cup.

The patriarchs

In the book of Genesis, Abraham, Isaac, Jacob, and Joseph are seen as the patriarchs, or "founding fathers," of what was to become Israel. Archeology has provided a wealth of information about the time in which their stories are set. The patriarchal stories may have happened between about 2600 and 1800 BCE, with the tales of Abraham being the earliest. Traditionally, Abraham, is said to have traveled from Ur in Iraq to Canaan, via Harran in Turkey.

A gold shell-shaped cosmetic container, used in Ur about 4,000 years ago

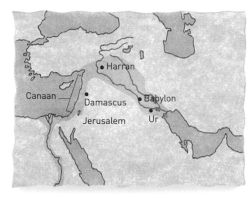

Patriarchs' path
This map shows the areas (in green) between which the patriarchs traveled.

Royal riches
During the time of Abraham, Ur was a wealthy city. Many of the graves excavated there in the 1920s contained expensive gifts for the afterlife, such as this ceremonial baton decorated with gold (above).

Golden glory
Expensive items such as this fine gold chalice (left) were found in the graves of Ur's royal family.

Temple tower
One of the most important buildings in Ur was the ziggurat, a type of tower built of mud bricks, with a temple on top. The biblical Tower of Babel (in the city of Babylon) would have been a similar structure.

Tunic made of colored and embroidered wool

Simple bow

Lyre

Bellows used by metal-workers

Duck-billed axe (see p. 47)

Donkey, one of the earliest beasts of burden

Women wear shoes, in contrast to the men's sandals

Patriarchal pot?

Finely made pottery goblets like this one (above) were common in northern Syria during the time of the patriarchs.

Gold decoration

Lapis lazuli inlay

For the dead

In Canaan, the dead were often buried in deep chambers entered by vertical shafts. Items of jewelry, such as this necklace from Jordan (above), were sometimes buried with the body.

Yogurt-maker

These vessels from Jordan (above) are thought to have been used for making yogurt (known as "leben").

Drinker's delight

This unusual flask from North Syria (above) was a device for raising liquid. Fluid entered through holes in the base, and could be retained by clamping a thumb over the narrow mouth. The liquid could then be released by removing the thumb pressure.

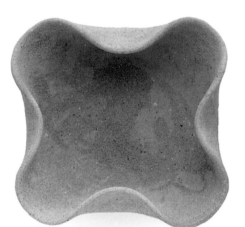

Fishy flame

The people of Canaan used fish oil in their lamps.

Sickle sword   *Wool kilt*   *Group's leader is called Absha*

Wall paintings

The stories of Joseph's adventures in Egypt are thought to have taken place between 2000 and 1800 BCE. These Egyptian wall paintings show a group of Asiatic people, probably Canaanites, being introduced to the Egyptian court.

Egypt

Lost and found
According to the Bible, Moses was found in the bulrushes.

In the Middle Bronze Age, groups of Canaanites moved to the Egyptian Delta and founded a dynasty called the Hyksos. Around 1550 BCE, the Egyptians expelled the Hyksos and regained control of Canaan. Egypt imposed heavy taxes on Canaan, but, in return, the Canaanite cities gained security. In the reign of pharaoh Ramesses II (1279–1213 BCE), many Canaanites were made homeless and migrated to the Judean hills. These dispossessed people, known to the Egyptians as Hapiru (or Hebrews), formed the basis of what was to become Israel.

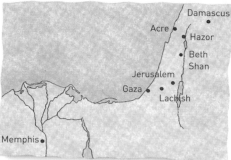

Egypt and Canaan
In the Late Bronze Age, Egypt took control of Canaan. Some Canaanite cities, such as Gaza, prospered under Egyptian rule.

Power symbol
This Egyptian ceremonial ax (left) has an elaborate openwork head.

Letter to the pharaoh
The Armana letters (above) were written by local rulers to the pharaoh Amenophis III. Some mention trouble caused by lawless bands of "Hapiru," homeless peoples living on the fringes of cities.

Stronghold
Beth Shan was one of the major centers of Egyptian control in Canaan. During the time of Ramesses II, the city was strongly fortified and had an Egyptian governor.

Hebrew slaves?
Both the Bible and an Egyptian papyrus mention Hapiru working for Ramesses II. Although this 19th-century painting suggests they were slaves, that might not have been the case.

The Philistines

In Ramesses III's reign (1187–1156 BCE), the Egyptian empire was threatened by fierce invaders from the Aegean. Known as the Sea Peoples, they included the Philistines. Ramesses pushed them back from the shores of Egypt in a great naval battle, but he could not stop them from settling in Canaan, at the southern end of the coastal strip.

Fine feathers
Philistine warriors wore feathered headdresses.

Philistine face
The Philistines, like some of the other Sea Peoples, buried their dead in distinctive "slipper-shaped" coffins. The lids, such as the one above, show rather grotesque human features.

Successful ruler
Ramesses II brought Egypt's long conflict with the Hittites to an end. After fighting the Hittites at the Battle of Qadesh in 1289 BCE, the Egyptians signed a peace treaty that brought them a period of peace and prosperity.

Striped headcloth indicates kingship

During the reign of Ramesses II, the number of hill-farming settlements in Judea increased dramatically.

Parting of the waters
Archeology cannot confirm the story of the Hebrew Exodus through the waters of the Red Sea. However, it is not unlikely that a group of Hapiru left Egypt during the reign of Ramesses II and found its way to the Judean hill country.

Mound life

Portrait of a Canaanite, a Late Bronze Age ivory from Lachish

The people of the Middle and Late Bronze Ages in Palestine are traditionally known as the Canaanites. But the distinctive Canaanite culture developed gradually, and its origins can be traced back to the 4th millennium BCE. New groups of people entering the country around 3200 BCE settled in sites chosen for their natural resources and access to trade routes. As generation after generation lived and built upon the same spot, huge artificial mounds of debris (household garbage and the foundations of old houses) built up. These mounds, still visible today, are known as tells.

Canaanite pottery of the Early Bronze Age, like this pitcher, is elegant and well made.

A cross-section through the tell reveals walls, floors, layers of ash and garbage, pits, and other features that show the site's history of occupation

The Citadel in Aleppo, Syria, is a tell that has been occupied continuously until quite recently.

What does it tell us?
A tell provides the archeologist with invaluable information about the past. Much of it consists of layers of mud bricks, the standard building material of the Holy Land. This material can show the archeologist the history of the site's occupation in reverse order. The model tell (above) is based on Tell Deir 'Alia, Jordan, the biblical city of Succoth.

Mounting defenses
By the Middle Bronze Age, many tell sites were becoming unstable. So the inhabitants strengthened the sides and added a coat of plaster to them. This created a smooth, defensive slope called a "glacis." The base of the glacis was held by a strong wall, and a ditch around the base of the mound completed the defenses. Elaborate gateways, like this one at Tell Dan in Israel, were built into the walls.

The city of Lachish
This reconstruction of Lachish (above) shows the tell as it might have been at the time of the siege in 701 BCE (see p. 46). The two walls are clearly visible, as is the strongly fortified gateway.

Faience jar
This jar (above), found at Lachish, is made of a glazed ceramic called faience.

Ledge handles typical of Canaanite pottery of this period

Pourer
The highly burnished finish of this pot (above) is called "red slip." This was a popular treatment for Early Bronze Age tablewares. The pot has a spout for pouring and ledge handles

Mud-brick buildings are often difficult to distinguish from surrounding soil

Houses with wall paintings

The Canaanites

Canaanite culture was at its peak in the Middle Bronze Age (c.2000–1550 BCE). During this period, the country developed extensive trade networks with Egypt, Syria, Anatolia, and Cyprus. Canaan's arts and crafts reached new levels of sophistication as its artists were influenced by a variety of sources. During the Late Bronze Age (1550–1150 BCE), Egypt dominated Canaan, bringing with it even more far-reaching trade links, including those with the Mycenaean people of Greece. But the local culture, by now well established, continued to flourish.

The land of Canaan
We do not know exactly how Palestine was governed during the Middle Bronze Age. It was probably made up of a large number of independent city-states, each ruled by a prince. Each city would have controlled its own area of land containing a number of dependent towns and villages.

Star attraction
This finely made star pendant (above) shows the skill of the Canaanite goldsmiths of the 16th century BCE.

Pots and palms
Canaanite pots of the Late Bronze Age are often decorated with this motif of palm trees and ibexes (left).

Dipper
"Dippers," such as the one shown here (left), were little pitchers used to take liquid out of a larger vessel.

Pilgrim's pleasure
This amusing pilgrim flask (above), dating to the end of the Late Bronze Age, has its own built-in drinking cup.

Sign with style
Egyptian-style seals and scarabs (seals in the shape of a beetle), were used to show ownership. Many were made by Canaanite craftsmen, and some were even imported to Egypt.

King riding on chariot

King seated on throne decorated with sphinxes

Kingly splendor
This carved ivory plaque from Megiddo (above) shows a Canaanite king on his throne receiving a victory procession. The king is also shown in his chariot.

Bull market
This bull vessel was imported from Cyprus.

A leg to stand on
This bronze figure shows a disabled Canaanite who has lost part of his left leg.

Foreign flowers
The Egyptian influence on Canaan was very strong toward the end of the Late Bronze Age. This necklace, from Tell es-Sa'idiyeh, has beads made of carnelian in the shape of Egyptian lotus flower seed pods.

City mound
The sites of many Canaanite city mounds, or tells (see pp. 14–15), are still visible in the Holy Land.

Carnelian bead

Whose head?
Dating to the 13th century BCE, this head from Lachish (above) shows strong Egyptian features.

Costly import
In the Late Bronze Age, high-quality pottery was imported to Canaan from Mycenae. Pots such as this one (left) were used to hold expensive perfumed oils.

Death and burial

Ancient people always treated their dead with great care. In the Holy Land, this often involved producing elaborate graves, sometimes dug deeply into rock. From the earliest times, the dead were buried with grave goods (items needed for the afterlife), such as jewelry, pottery, tools, and weapons. Excavating burial sites provides archeologists with a rich source of information about the people themselves—their beliefs, the objects they used, and their physical characteristics. The objects shown here come from a child's grave, excavated at Tell es-Sa'idiyeh, Jordan.

Fastener
This pin fastened the girl's shroud (burial cloth).

Bracelet
The girl wore a bracelet of carnelian and silver beads on her left wrist.

A silver finger ring was worn on the left hand.

Lucky charm?
This soapstone ring was found on the girl's chest. It may have been worn as a necklace.

One by one
People often wore single earrings. This one (right), found beneath the skull, was probably worn on the left ear.

Fine decoration
Bronze bangles were worn as jewelry throughout the Iron Age. These bangles, with their delicate decoration, were worn as anklets.

On the head
This clasp (right) was found on top of the skull. It may have been fixed to a cap, perhaps to attach a tassel.

Decoration on the end of the bangle

Grooves to hold thread

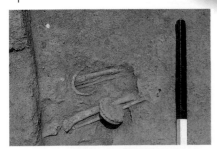

The anklets in position
This detail of the girl's lower legs shows the bronze anklets in the position in which they were found.

Finery

The girl buried in this grave clearly came from a wealthy family. Her beautiful necklace (below) is made up of finely worked silver and carnelian beads with a central group made of agate.

Silver beads are finely granulated (see p. 43)

Strainer

Spout

Just for fun?

This finely decorated bronze spindle (left) is an unusual burial gift. Perhaps spinning was one of the child's favorite pastimes.

Feeding bottle

This pot (above), in the shape of an animal (perhaps a calf), is the most moving item in the grave. It has a strainer in the top and a hole through the snout, and may well have been a feeding bottle. It was slightly broken when put into the grave, and was probably much loved—a bit like a teddy bear with a missing ear.

Simple shells

A bracelet of tiny white shell beads (right) was worn on the girl's right wrist.

A girl's burial

The objects on this page come from the grave of a seven-year-old girl. She was buried in a simple pit, wrapped in a white linen shroud. This photograph shows many of the grave goods in position.

Mark of status

The inclusion of a seal showing a bull and a winged symbol (left), reflects the high status of the girl's family.

Delicate ivory furniture ornament from Samaria

The Israelites

After the Egyptians left Canaan, the Israelites and the Philistines lived side by side for nearly 100 years. But in the 11th century BCE, the Philistines tried to extend their territory. Faced with this threat, the Israelites united as one nation, with Saul as their leader. In about 1000 BCE, Saul's son David was proclaimed king of the Israelite nation. He defeated the Philistines and expanded Israel's territory. The kingdom continued to flourish under David's son Solomon, who built the great Temple in Jerusalem.

After Solomon's death, in 928 BCE, the kingdom split in two, with Judah in the south and Israel in the north.

No smoke without fire
This lively 19th-century engraving (above) shows the destruction of the Temple by the Babylonians in 587 BCE.

The divided kingdoms
This map (above) shows the two kingdoms. The capital of Judah in the south was Jerusalem, while the capital of Israel in the north was Samaria.

First mention of Israel
This stela (above) of the pharaoh Merneptah (1213–1203 BCE) records a military campaign in Canaan against Gezer, Ashkelon, and Israel. This is the first recorded mention of Israel.

Bronze columns called Jachin and Boaz

Porch

Lion's hindquarters
This ivory fragment (left) is from King Ahab's palace at Samaria. Israel and Phoenicia had close relations; Phoenician artists were often used for fine work such as this.

Solomon's Temple

Wealth from trade enabled Solomon to carry out large-scale building projects. The most important project was the Temple in Jerusalem. No traces of the building are left, but there are detailed descriptions of it in the Bible. This evidence has helped us to create reconstructions of the Temple, such as the one shown below.

Solomon

Sphinxes or cherubim?
The "cherubim" mentioned in the Bible were winged sphinxes (human-headed lions).

Main hall lined with cedar

Holy of Holies, with cedar panels and inlaid with gold

"Cherubim" (sphinxes) flanking Ark

Raised platform

This elegant Judean decanter, used for serving wine or water, dates to the 8th century BCE.

King's mark
The Judean royal winged scarab symbol, together with the name "Socoh," are stamped on this jar (right). Socoh was an administrative center in Judah.

This imaginative 19th-century view shows the construction of Solomon's Temple.

The Phoenicians

The Phoenician writing on this seal identifies its owner as "Tamak-el, son of Milkam.".

By the 2nd millennium BCE, the Israelites occupied most of Palestine except for the southern coastal strip, which was held by the Philistines. To the north, the Aramaean kingdoms controlled most of central and northern Syria. The remaining Canaanite territory, in the northwest, became Phoenicia. With little farming land, the Phoenicians turned to the sea to make a living, becoming great seafarers and traders. They were also excellent craft workers, whose work was in demand all over the Middle East.

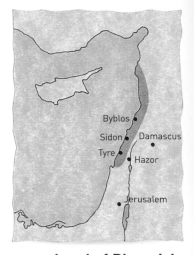

Land of Phoenicia
Most Phoenicians lived near the coastal cities of Byblos, Tyre, and Sidon (area in red).

Painted pot
Vessels such as this elegant, painted pitcher (right), were traded throughout the eastern Mediterranean.

Sphinx

Geometric design

Mixed motifs
The much-traveled Phoenicians produced art that blended a variety of styles. This bronze bowl (above) combines Egyptian sphinxes with Syrian geometric designs.

Fast mover
This Assyrian relief (right) shows a Phoenician ship called a bireme. The two banks of oars on either side increased the ship's speed.

Trading post
Phoenician traders set up colonies around the Mediterranean. The city of Carthage in Tunisia was founded by settlers from Tyre in about 814 BCE.

Brittle but beautiful
The Phoenicians were skilled glass-makers. Finely ground sand was mixed with soda and pigments. When heated, the mixture fused to form colored glass, such as in the example above.

Precious booty
This piece of carved ivory (right) was found at Nimrud, the Assyrian capital. It was probably brought there as tribute (see p. 48).

(see p. 48)

Shaping up
Glassblowing had not yet been invented, so vessels were made by molding the glass paste around a clay core.

Shields

Port of call
The Phoenicians created large ports capable of handling international shipping. The image above is a modern view of Byblos, one of the busiest Phoenician ports.

Double ranks of oars

Inscription reads "Arrowhead of 'Ada', son of Ba'la'"

Phoenician alphabet
The Canaanites probably invented the first alphabet in the Middle Bronze Age. But the Phoenicians refined and developed the system, and some of their letters appear on this arrowhead. Their 22-letter alphabet formed the basis of the Greek alphabet, and, ultimately, that of the Romans.

Religion

Until the Israelite concept of the "One God" became widely accepted, the Canaanites worshiped a variety of gods and goddesses. These dominated every aspect of life, such as weather, war, and the harvest. Most of what we know about these gods comes from a collection of clay tablets, dating to the Late Bronze Age, found at Ras Shamra in Syria.

Early god?
This lime-plaster statue (above) was found at 'Ain Ghazal. It may have represented an early god.

Fertility figure
This gold plaque (above) shows Astarte, the Canaanite goddess of fertility. Dating to the 16th century BCE, it was found at Tell el-'Ajjûl.

Warrior god
This figure (right) dates to the Late Bronze Age. It is thought to represent the god Baal, who is often depicted as a warrior.

Popular deity
This terra-cotta plaque from Alalakh (left) depicts Astarte, the most powerful and popular Canaanite goddess.

Baal's prophets
The prophet Elijah asked God to light a sacrificial fire to prove His superiority over the Canaanite god Baal.

By the light of the moon
This Canaanite temple at Hazor (left) was dedicated to the Moon god and his wife.

Eye of Horus
The eye of Horus was one of the most popular Egyptian amulets (charms). It represents the sky-god Horus.

Whose hand?
This finely carved ivory hand (left) was all that remained of the statue of an unknown god or goddess. It was excavated from the "Fosse" temple at Lachish.

God of wine
This bust of the Nabataean (Arab) wine god Dushara (above) is from the temple of Dushara at Si'a in southern Syria.

The facade of the temple at Jerusalem depicted on a coin of Simon bar Kochba.

Astarte model
Despite Israelite laws banning the worship of other gods, models of Canaanite deities, such as the one above, continued to be produced during the Iron Age.

Gods of Egypt
Egyptian amulets appeared in the Late Bronze Age, when Canaan was ruled by Egypt. These amulets (left) show the sphinx, with a cat's body and a woman's head, and Sekhmet, goddess of the burning Sun.

| Sekhmet | Sekhmet | Sphinx | Sekhmet |

Greek goddess Aphrodite
The Greek domination of Syria and Palestine after 332 BCE brought with it the Greek religion, with its various gods and goddesses.

Food and crops

Milk and honey
In Moses's time, Canaan was a richly fertile place with a long history of agriculture.

Perhaps the most important advance made by early people was the development of agriculture. In the Holy Land, this happened in about 8000 BCE. The process began with the selection of plants and animals that were suitable for cultivation and rearing. These species were then bred selectively over hundreds of years, until they became suited to the needs of humans. Early farmers grew wheat, barley, and a variety of fruits and vegetables.

Mortar and pestle from the Iron Age

From the pharmacy
Herbs such as cumin were grown not only as flavorings, but also for their medicinal value.

Favored for flavor
The book of Numbers records how the Israelites of the Exodus remembered with longing the fruits and vegetables they had left behind in Egypt. These included leeks, onions, and garlic. These vegetables are still valued for their distinctive flavorings today.

Scallions

Leeks

Lentils
Lentils were grown from at least the 7th millennium BCE. They could be used in soups and pastes, or be combined with grains and ground into flour to make cakes.

Blowing in the wind
After harvesting, cereals were tossed in the air to allow the lighter chaff to blow away. The heavy grains were left behind.

On the terraces
Terrace agriculture is a comparatively recent form of cultivation on hillside sites in the Holy Land.

Barley
Barley was one of the earliest cereals to be cultivated. It was used to make bread and beer.

Early crop
Although millet was grown in Mesopotamia from at least 3000 BCE, it does not seem to have been an important crop in the Holy Land until post-Roman times.

Working with wheat
The earliest varieties of cultivated wheat were emmer and einkorn. By biblical times, these cereals had been replaced as the main field crop by durum wheat. This species made excellent flour for bread.

Cutter
Cutting edge

Iron sickles were common during the 1st millennium BCE.

Sickles
Flint blades (left) were set in wooden or bone handles to make sickles for harvesting cereal crops. They often had toothed edges.

Continued on next page

Continued from previous page

Through the groves
This Assyrian relief (left) shows a group of Chaldean prisoners being led through the palm groves of southern Iraq.

Garden of Eden
This painting (right) by Roelandt Jacobsz Savery (1576–1639) shows the story of the Garden of Eden. It depicts the rich variety of the natural world.

Foreign fruit
Apples were probably introduced to the Holy Land from Syria or Turkey in about 4000 BCE.

Cinnamon

Spice of life
The Old Testament often refers to spices. Joseph was sold by his brothers to Ishmaelite spice-merchants bound for Egypt.

Major export
The olive tree, native to the Syria–Palestine region, was an important natural resource. Olive oil (used in cooking, medicine, and as a fuel) became a major export.

Fresh figs

Early fruit
Figs were well established in the Holy Land by about 5000 BCE.

Dried figs

Compressed dried figs

Standby
Dried figs could be kept for months, providing a useful food supply when other foods were scarce.

Pocket snack
Figs could also be pressed and made into cakes. These formed a source of nutritious food on long journeys.

Olive oil
Olive oil was kept in large storage jars, but it would have been served at the table in small pitchers, like this one (left).

Prized specimen
The acacia is one of the few trees to grow in the Sinai desert. Its wood was used to build the Ark of the Covenant.

Popular proteins
The most popular nuts were almonds and pistachios; they are the only nuts mentioned in the Bible.

Pistachios

Date harvest
This relief from Tell Halaf in Syria (above) shows a man using a ladder to gather dates.

Almonds

Pomegranate
This fruit, prized for its bittersweet juice, was established in the Holy Land by the Middle Bronze Age.

The olive seems to have been cultivated from at least 4000 BCE, not only for its delicious fruit, but also for its highly prized oil.

Fruit of Jericho
The date palm grew abundantly throughout the Fertile Crescent. Jericho is referred to in the Old Testament as the "city of palm trees," and the Jericho date was a well-known variety.

Continued on next page

Continued from previous page

The importance of fish to the people living by the Sea of Galilee is mentioned in many biblical stories.

Fishing

Fish was one of the earliest sources of food in the Holy Land. The Assyrians kept supplies of fish in specially made lakes, known as "vivaria."

Hooked

This bronze fish hook (right) from Tell es-Sa'idiyeh may have been used to fish in the Jordan River.

Multipurpose

Grapes could be dried and preserved as raisins to be eaten out of season.

Fresh grapes provided a popular and refreshing fruit.

Modern golden raisins

Masters of wine

Wealthy Canaanites of the Late Bronze Age had bronze wine sets of a small pitcher to draw the wine, a strainer for filtering, and a bowl to drink from.

Strainer

Pitcher

Drinking bowl

This painting shows the importance of mealtimes in early cultures.

Wine-making

As cities developed in the 3rd millennium BCE, the now-settled communities of the Levant began to grow additional crops, such as grapes. Vines were widely grown, not only for their fresh fruit, but also for wine-making, and Palestine became renowned for its wines.

This painting by Caravaggio shows Jesus revealing himself to two of his disciples after the Resurrection.

Enter the chicken

The chicken was domesticated in northern India, some time before 2000 BCE. It was familiar in Egypt by 1400 BCE, but we do not know when it arrived in Palestine.

Cheese was made from cow, goat, or sheep milk.

Thirst quencher

The watermelon was probably eaten in Palestine from the beginning of the Middle Bronze Age. It provided a source of water during dry periods.

Watermelon seeds could be eaten as a food.

Whisked away

This unusual bronze object (left) was found in the "Fosse Temple" at Lachish. It was probably a food whisk.

Plates to eat

Circular flaps of unleavened bread (made without yeast) were created by slapping the dough against the inside wall of a cylindrical oven, or "tannur."

Fowl food

Fish was a more common food than fowl, although people living in the Jordan hills may well have eaten desert partridges.

Cucumbers were probably introduced into Palestine during the 2nd millennium BCE, by which time they were a common food in Egypt.

Egging them on

The eggs of birds were valuable foodstuffs. Ostrich eggs, frequently shown in Egyptian paintings, were especially prized. The hen's eggs shown above are far smaller, but are just as nutritious.

Ancient Canaanite vessel

Animals

Many of the animals that once roamed the Holy Land have now disappeared. Lions, ostriches, and crocodiles, all mentioned in the Bible, have been hunted to extinction in the region. Before the development of agriculture, animals were hunted for food and skins. Later, people kept them for wool and dairy produce. The first animals to be domesticated, during the Stone Age, were sheep and goats. In the following Chalcolithic period, pigs and cattle were being reared as well.

The scarab beetle was held sacred by the Egyptians.

Jesus as the "Good Shepherd" from a 19th-century engraving

This painting by Hans Jordaens shows the story of Noah and the ark. God told Noah to take two of every living thing into the ark to save them from the coming flood.

Hollow snout, indicating that this vessel may have been a feeding bottle

Popular plaything
This Iron Age pottery cow from Lachish (left) might have been a child's toy. It could also have been a feeding bottle, since it has a hole in the top and a hollow snout to drink through.

The Nubian ibex is the "wild goat" of the Bible. It is still found in some rocky areas today.

32

Monkey business
Apes were imported from Africa in Solomon's reign.

What, a boar?
Wild boars, like the one on this amulet from Lachish (above), are still found in the Jordan Valley.

Samson and the lion
This illustration shows Samson's biblical fight with the lion. Lions were once common in Palestine.

Payment to the king
The Black Obelisk in Nimrud (above) commemorates 31 military campaigns of the Assyrian king Shalmaneser III. It shows some of the tribute paid to the king by the ruler of Sukha in Syria, including two lions and a deer.

Bears in the woods
Small, pale-coated Syrian bears lived in the hills of Palestine until very recently.

Spotted cat
Leopards were common in Palestine in biblical times. One was last seen at Ein Gedi, near the Dead Sea, in 1974.

Out for a duck
This ivory duck from Lachish (right) was probably the decorative end of a cosmetic spoon.

In the stable
The importance of meat- and milk-producing animals is shown in engravings, like this nativity scene by Gustave Doré.

The wise men
The three wise men ride one-humped Arabian camels, which were domesticated in Egypt before 3000 BCE and were familiar in Palestine by 1500 BCE.

Clothing

The earliest people probably clothed themselves in animal skins. Spinning and weaving date back to at least the 7th millennium BCE, as shown by a remarkable discovery of preserved material at Naha Hemar in the Judean Desert. Later, people made clothes from a variety of materials, colored with natural dyes. Shoes and hats were usually made from leather and felt.

High and mighty
This depiction of a rich woman of the 10th century BCE (above) wears an elaborate headdress.

Egyptian influence
This Phoenician ivory panel (above) shows a figure wearing royal, Egyptian-style garments.

Weaving tools
It is not clear how these bone weaving tools (left) were used. The spatula was probably slipped between the vertical threads on the loom to close up the horizontal threads.

Spatula

Point, or awl

Off-the-shoulder
These Israelites (above) wear skull caps, long kilts, and cloaks draped over one shoulder. The fringed kilts and cloaks were probably woven in brightly colored patterns.

Loom weight
This clay loom weight (below) was used to weigh down the vertical threads of the loom.

Spindle whorl

Rebekah
This painting (right) is of Isaac's wife Rebekah. It illustrates the 19th-century idea of Old Testament costume.

In a spin
To twist fibers together to make a single thread, people used a stick with a type of "fly wheel" on it. These objects (above) are called "spindle whorls."

Safety pin

After about 1000 BCE, pins called "fibulae" were used to fasten garments. This example (left) is Persian.

Buttoned up

Toggle pins (right) were early types of fasteners. The pin was attached by its "eye" to one side; a string was sewn on the other side. To fasten a garment, the string was wound around the pin.

Eye

Middle Bronze Age toggle pins

Pattern of original textile

Under the veil

The scene above shows the typical costume of Judean women—a loose tunic and a long veil covering the hair.

Traces of textile

This bronze javelin from the 12th century BCE (right) was found in a grave at Tell es-Saʿidiyeh, Jordan. It had been wrapped in Egyptian linen.

Headgear

This delicate golden headband from Tell el-ʿAjjûl (left) dates back to the 16th century BCE.

Sandal

This sandal (left) dates to the Roman period and was found at Masada (see p. 57). Such sandals were worn in the Holy Land from at least 2000 BCE.

Very fine, flexible metal

Roman sandal designs

Gold earrings from Lachish

Jewelry

The need to adorn the body using jewelry and cosmetics must have been felt from the very earliest times. In the hands of the Canaanite craftsmen of the Middle and Late Bronze Ages, jewelry became a highly accomplished art form. Goldsmiths used sophisticated techniques such as repoussée (raising the surface by hammering from behind) and granulation (the use of tiny grains of metal). The Israelites inherited these skills from the Phoenicians, whose jewelry was widely sought after.

Silver grains
This silver earring (right) has fine granulated decoration.

Earring
This Persian gold earring (left) is made up of hollow spheres.

Hair dressing
The finest hair combs were made of bone or ivory, and were often delicately carved.

For face painting
During the Early Bronze Age, hollowed-out and finely engraved animal bones, such as the one on the right, were used as containers for cosmetics such as eye makeup.

Pendants
These unusual bone pendants (left), dating to the Iron Age, were found at Lachish. They probably had some significance in addition to being decorative. The varying numbers of dot and circle patterns suggests that they might have been used as calendars or calculating devices.

Lengths of beaten bronze could be easily bent to the right size

Bangles and anklets were a popular form of jewelry in the Iron Age.

Necklace

Like most Canaanite necklaces, this one (above) was found without its original thread. The arrangement of the beads is, therefore, quite random.

Faience bead

Blue beads

During the Late Bronze Age, many beads were made of faience—a glazed material consisting mainly of quartz.

Holy offering

A number of gold pendants (above) were found in the "Fosse Temple," a Late Bronze Age Canaanite sanctuary at Lachish, They probably formed part of an offering to a god or goddess.

Decoration is formed when gold is beaten over a patterned object

Touch of glamour

Jewelry worn by actress Vivien Leigh in her role as Cleopatra was based on Middle Eastern originals.

Traces of linen in which bowl was wrapped

Egyptian plants

Many Late Bronze Age objects were influenced by Egypt. The palmettes on this necklace (above) are a typical motif.

Palmette

Below the belt

The lower part of this Iron Age terracotta figure (left) clearly shows two pairs of anklets.

Fish out of water

Toward the end of the Late Bronze Age, many objects made in Egypt were imported into Canaan. This fine ivory cosmetic box in the shape of a fish (right) was found inside the bronze bowl in a grave at Tell es-Sa'idiyeh.

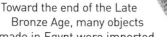

Money and trade

This Phoenician glass vessel was found at Amathus, Cyprus.

The growth of cities saw trade begin to flourish in the 3rd millennium BCE. Merchants carried their wares between Egypt and Arabia in the south, and Anatolia and Mesopotamia in the north. Cereals, flour, oil, and wine were exported to foreign markets from Palestine. Canaanite art and craft objects were also exported widely. In return, raw materials, such as wood and metal, were imported from abroad.

Weighing them up
Before coins were invented, goods were bought and sold using a variety of materials, such as metal ingots. These had to be weighed to assess what they were worth. So accurate weights were needed, such as these lion-shaped ones from Assyria.

During their first revolt against Rome in 66 CE (see p. 55), the Jews created their own coins.

Wagon train
A pottery model of a covered wagon (right) from Hamman, Syria, shows the type of vehicle that was used to transport goods in the late 3rd millennium BCE.

Shekel
The standard Jewish silver coin was the shekel (right), which was also a unit of weight. This coin was from the first Jewish revolt.

Stopping on the way
This painting by Edward Lear shows a desert caravan at Mount Sinai. It gives an idea of what long-distance travel must have been like in ancient times.

Coins
Coins came into use in the Holy Land at the time of Alexander the Great (see p. 54). This Roman coin (left) shows the emperor Vespasian.

One hump or two?
Two-humped Bactrian camels are featured on the Assyrian Black Obelisk (see p. 33). These creatures did not appear in the Holy Land until Solomon's time.

A coin of the second Jewish revolt bears the name of its leader Shimeon.

These coins from the second Jewish revolt (132–135 CE) bear inscriptions. The first reads "Year one of the redemption of Israel"; the second bears the name of Shimeon.

These coins from the reign of Herod Archelaus (4 BCE–6 CE) show a helmet and a bunch of grapes. The Greek inscription reads "Herod, governor of the people."

Poppy power
During the Late Bronze Age, little pitchers, such as the example above, known as "bil-bils," were imported into Canaan. They were used to hold the drug opium. The shape of the pitcher is strikingly similar to that of an upturned poppy head.

Continued on next page

A bronze coin from the time of
Agrippa I (37–44 CE)

Turning the tables
Jesus objected to trading by
the Temple in Jerusalem and
overthrew the stalls.

Ingot
Precious
metals such as
silver were frequently
traded as ingots.

Victory coin
This coin (right) records
the Roman victory
in the first Jewish
revolt (see p. 55).

(see p. 55)

*The "stirrup jar"
gets its name
from its handles*

Import
Beautifully
made Mycenaean
vessels, known as "stirrup jars,"
were imported into Canaan during
the Late Bronze Age.

Merchant ship
King Solomon was intent
upon developing a wide
network of sea trade
relations. With the help
of Hiram, king of Tyre,
he built a major port at
Ezion Geber, at the head
of the Red Sea. A joint
Israelite and Phoenician
fleet was based here,
and every three years
ships set sail for the
coast of East Africa in
search of fine gold.

Store jar
In the 12th century BCE,
Tell es-Saʻidiyeh, east of the
Jordan River, was an Egyptian
taxation and distribution center.
Egyptian jars found there in one of
the storerooms may have been used
to store and transport wine.

Sea horses

The most expensive wood came from the "Cedars of Lebanon." This Assyrian relief from the 8th century BCE (above) shows Phoenician ships hauling logs along the Syrian coast. The ships, known as "hippoi," had horse figureheads.

"Neseph", five-sixths of a shekel

8 shekels

"Beqa," half a shekel

How heavy?

The ancient Palestinian system of weights was based on the shekel (equivalent to about 0.4 oz/11.4 g). These stone weights (above) are inscribed in Hebrew with their value.

Long-distance trader

This Roman merchant ship, known as a "corbita," was used for long-distance shipping across the Mediterranean.

Lighting the way

Pharos, the lighthouse of Alexandria in Egypt, was one of the seven wonders of the ancient world.

Royal purple

One of the most sought-after items traded by Phoenician merchants was their purple-dyed cloth. In Roman times, it could only be worn by the emperor.

Their true colors

The highly prized purple dye was extracted from a gland of the murex snail. Processing required slow simmering for about two weeks. Up to 60,000 snails were needed for each pound of dye. Different tints were achieved by varying the amount of extract used.

Arts and crafts

Some of the earliest people of the Holy Land were highly skilled craftworkers, such as the Stone Age artists who made the lime-plaster statues found at 'Ain Ghazal, Jordan. Beautiful carved ivories and elaborate copper objects are found in the following Chalcolithic period. But it was the Canaanites of the Bronze Age and the Phoenicians of the Iron Age who turned this tradition of skillful work into a real industry.

For show
This ax head from the Middle Bronze Age (above) shows a lion fighting a dog. It was probably made for ceremonial use.

Daily life in ancient Jericho
Items of wooden furniture found preserved in tombs in Jericho show the skill and expertise of Canaanite carpenters.

Music makers
Dancing and music were popular pastimes. Instruments such as harps, flutes, trumpets, and a range of percussion instruments were used.

Carved alphabetic writing

Writing it down
Writing using alphabetic letters began in Canaan (see pp. 16–17). An early alphabetic script was found on this 17th-century BCE bronze dagger from Lachish (above).

Ivory queens
The Canaanites and Phoenicians were renowned for their ivory carving. Ivory was often used for inlays or as ornaments for furniture. This example (right) is a 9th-century BCE Phoenician ivory from the Assyrian city of Nimrud. It shows two seated queens in Egyptian style.

Hard to carve

The combat between a lion and a dog was a popular subject for the Canaanites. This example (left) from Beth Shan is carved on a piece of black basalt, a very hard stone that took great skill to work.

Most of the methods of the ancient potter are still used today.

Applied gold decoration

Syrian style

This ivory head of a female (above) was found at Nimrud. It might have been the work of a Syrian carver.

Granulation

Funny face

The finest pottery ever seen in Palestine was made by the Canaanites. This extraordinary face vase from Jericho (above) dates to the 6th century BCE.

Golden grains

This pendant from Tell el-'Ajjûl (left) is decorated by granulation. In this process, gold wire is melted to make tiny beads, which are then attached to the surface.

Carved in stone

Vessels carved from stones such as calcite and alabaster were often used as containers for perfumed oil. This example (left) comes from Tell es-Sa'idiyeh.

Treasures of the Temple

King Solomon asked the king of Tyre for Phoenician craftworkers when building his Temple in Jerusalem.

War and weapons

Until copper smelting was discovered some time before 4000 BCE, the people of the Holy Land made weapons out of wood, bone, and stone. As the Early Bronze Age cities grew, the techniques of warfare developed, and armies were established.

Mass-produced weapons such as swords, axes, and spears were made of copper, then bronze. The Philistines probably introduced ironworking into Canaan around 1200 BCE; after this, iron weapons gradually replaced bronze ones.

This relief shows an Aramaean cavalryman of the 9th century BCE. It comes from Tell Halaf.

Giant-slayer
One of the most ancient weapons was the sling, used to hurl clay bullets, or smooth, rounded pebbles at the enemy. The Bible recounts how David killed the Philistine leader Goliath using a sling.

Taking aim
This slinger (left) is depicted on a 9th-century BCE relief from the royal palace at Tell Halaf, Syria.

Pair of helmets from the Persian period.

Good grip
The hilt (handle) of this Late Bronze Age dagger from Syria (above), has deep grooves to allow a wooden or bone grip to be inserted.

Broad cutting blade

Sword would have been attached to wooden or bone hilt with copper rivets

Ridge to make blade stronger

Spear

During the Middle Bronze Age, spear and javelin heads were made with a hollow socket into which a shaft could be inserted.

Socket

Ax man

This Middle Bronze Age warrior figure (left), dating to about 1800 BCE, holds a distinctive ax with a head shaped rather like a duck's bill.

Ax

Sickle sword

Shield

This archer's bow is made of layers of wood, glue, and horn.

Armed to the teeth

This Middle Bronze Age warrior (right) holds a spear and a "sickle sword." One of the Canaanites on the Egyptian Beni Hasan wall paintings (see pp. 10–11) is shown holding this type of sword.

Roman soldier

During the Roman period, a highly organized army helped the emperors keep control of their vast territories.

Tang for attaching to shaft

Early Bronze Age javelin

Copper javelins with long "tangs" were tied to their shafts with leather thongs.

Horsepower

The Canaanites used horse chariots as light and fast fighting vehicles.

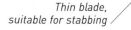

Thin blade, suitable for stabbing

Heavyweight weapon

During the time of the patriarchs (see pp. 10–11), metal weapons became larger and heavier. This sword (above) from Beit Dagin, near Tel Aviv, is one of the largest known weapons of this period.

Continued on next page

The siege of Lachish

The northern kingdom of Israel came to an end in 722 BCE when the Assyrians captured Samaria. The southern kingdom of Judah, ruled by Hezekiah (715–687 BCE), was also forced to submit. In 701 BCE, Assyria's king Sennacherib swept into Judah, destroying many cities, including Lachish. The siege and capture of this city are depicted in a series of limestone reliefs from Sennacherib's palace at Nineveh. The Assyrians finally advanced on Jerusalem, where Hezekiah was forced to pay heavy tribute.

This painting by 19th-century artist William Dyce shows Joash, son of Shemaah, who was one of David's heroes.

Flaming torches thrown down by the defenders

Arrowheads
Bronze arrowheads were used from 2000 BCE. Iron ones came in after about 1100 BCE.

Selection of five bronze arrowheads

Ladder, used by the Assyrians for scaling, but pushed down by the defenders

Down with the walls
The battering ram may have been developed as early as the Middle Bronze Age. It was used to attack defensive walls until explosives were invented.

Iron arrowhead

Battering ram—the soldier at the front is pouring water over the front of the machine to prevent it from catching fire

Tortoise shell
The Romans used stout swords and big rectangular shields. Soldiers locked their shields together to form a solid wall or roof—a formation known as a *testudo*, or tortoise.

Battle-axes

Toward the end of the 3rd millennium BCE, battle-axes were secured to a handle by means of a socket. They were used to pierce helmets—and crack skulls!

Ax head with handle

Duck's bill

During the Middle Bronze Age, ax blades were made longer, to produce the so-called "duck-billed" ax (left).

Parapet of round shields on top of city gatehouse

Judaean archers and slingers defending the gatehouse

Large hooded shield

Assyrian archer – the pointed helmet was effective protection against vertically falling showers of arrows

Assyrian spearman with crested helmet

Siege ramps of banked-up earth covered with logs

Deportees leaving the gate, bound for exile in Assyria, carrying with them a few possessions in bags

Bronze scale armor like this was worn by the Assyrians during the siege of Lachish.

A 19th-century drawing of scale armor.

This Roman catapult could hurl rocks over long distances.

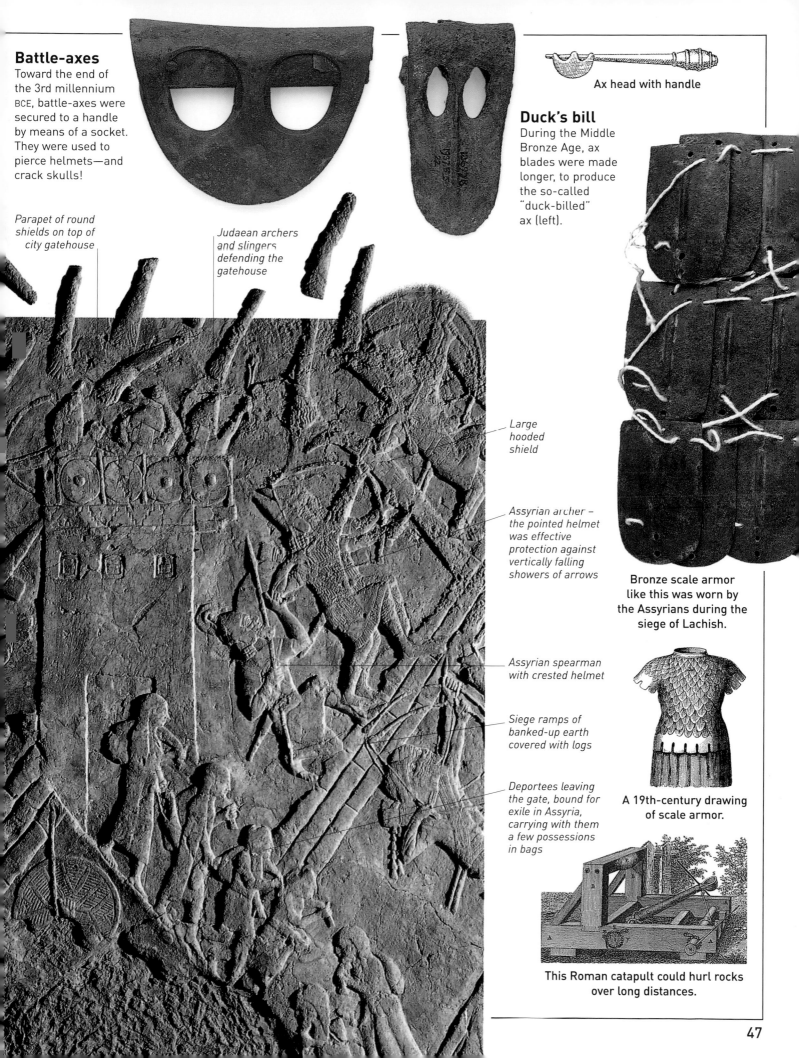

The Assyrians

The kingdom of Assyria was centered on the valley of the River Tigris in present-day Iraq. It had existed since at least 2000 BCE. During the 9th century BCE, the Assyrian kings began to expand their territory. The next 200 years saw the relentless advance of Assyrian armies against Phoenicia, Syria, and, ultimately, Israel and Judah. In 722 BCE, the northern kingdom of Israel came to an end when its capital, Samaria, fell to the Assyrians. Judah survived longer, but only by paying crippling tribute (taxes in the form of treasures or other goods). Many of the exploits of the Assyrians are shown on carved stone slabs made to adorn the royal palaces.

Household god
The figure above is of the Assyrian god Lahmu, "the hairy."

Heroic struggle
In spite of their warlike image, the Assyrians appreciated art and fine craftsmanship. This ivory plaque (left) shows an Assyrian hero fighting a lion.

The empire's spread
At its greatest extent, in the early 7th century BCE, the Assyrian empire covered a vast area, stretching from Iran to Egypt.

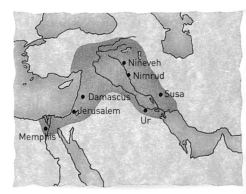

Bottle

Cup

For home and palace
This elegant, thin-walled cup (left) is an example of "Assyrian palace ware." On the right is a small bottle, beautifully decorated in multicolored glaze.

War goddess
This bronze plaque (right) shows Ishtar, the most important goddess of the Assyrians. Here she is shown as the goddess of war, mounted on her favored animal, the lion. Ishtar was the equivalent of the Canaanite goddess Astarte (see pp. 24–25).

Winged goddess

This blue plaque (right), from the 9th century BCE, comes from the temple of Ninurta at Nimrud. The winged goddess is probably Ishtar.

Blue color typical of Assyrian decorative wares

Tribute from Phoenicia

This ivory panel (above) from the Assyrian capital Nimrud was made by a Phoenician craftsman. It was probably brought back as tribute in the 8th century BCE.

Payments to the king

The military campaigns of Assyrian king Shalmaneser III (858–824 BCE) were commemorated on a monument known as the Black Obelisk in Nimrud. One of the scenes (above) shows Jehu, king of Israel, giving tribute to Shalmaneser.

Lion's share

Lions were a popular subject in Assyrian art. This example (above) might originally have been attached to the handle of a fan.

Making your mark

Small stone cylinders were carved with a design and rolled out on clay tablets. The resulting impression acted as a signature or mark of ownership. This seal (above), dating to around 750 BCE, shows a heroic figure grasping two ostriches by the neck.

State room

Shown here is a 19th-century reconstruction of the richly decorated throne room of King Ashurnasirpal II at Nimrud. The carved reliefs were originally painted in bright colors.

The Babylonians

Hebrew seal of the Chaldean period

In the 2nd millennium BCE, a people known as the Amorites founded a dynasty at the city of Babylon in Mesopotamia. In the 18th century BCE, the Babylonians, under King Hammurabi, ruled over the whole of Mesopotamia. This "Old Babylonian" period ended when the Hittite king Mursilis I attacked Babylonia in 1595 BCE and destroyed the city of Babylon. In the 7th century BCE, the city's fortunes improved when Nabopolassar assumed kingship of Babylon and founded the Chaldean dynasty.

Stone maceheads were often placed in temples. This one is dedicated to Nergal, the god of disease.

Builder
Bronze figures showing a king carrying a basket of building materials were placed in temples.

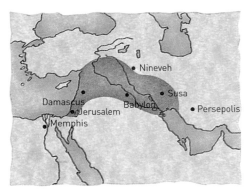

Nabopolassar's empire
In 612 BCE, Nabopolassar overthrew the Assyrians and laid claim to their lands, including Judah. His son Nebuchadnezzar II raided Judah in 597 BCE after a rebellion.

Aquarius
The Babylonians are thought to have invented the zodiac. This plaque (left) shows an ancestor of the water-bearer Aquarius.

Painting of Babylon's ziggurat by Pieter Bruegel the Elder.

Great gate
Nebuchadnezzar II rebuilt Babylon. One of his most impressive buildings was the Ishtar Gate (above).

Tower or temple?
According to the book of Genesis, the Tower of Babel was built by the descendants of Noah in order to reach Heaven. This is a reference to Babylon's ziggurat, or temple-tower.

On the boundary

In the Old Babylonian period, contracts relating to land and tax were often recorded on a carved stone known as a boundary stone. The symbols on the stone represent the gods and goddesses who witnessed the contract.

Snake symbol of the underworld god Ishtaran

Moon, representing the Moon god Sin

Sun, representing the Sun god Shamash

Planet Venus, representing the goddess Ishtar

Nabu, god of writing, seen here as a wedge-shaped (cuneiform) symbol

Headdresses representing sky gods Ann and Enlil

Scorpion, symbol of the goddess Ishhara

Altars and shrines

51

The Persians

Wealthy or important people sewed ornaments like this on to their clothes.

During the 2nd millennium BCE, the Persians settled in Parsa (now Fars in present-day Iran). Their early history is linked to that of the Medes, who settled in the same region. In 550 BCE, Cyrus the Great deposed his grandfather, the Median king Astyages. Cyrus founded the Achaemenid empire and became the undisputed ruler of both the Medes and the Persians. In 539 BCE, Cyrus defeated Babylonia, inheriting its empire, which included Syria and Palestine. It was during the reign of Cyrus that the Jews were allowed to return to Palestine.

This glazed brick frieze from Susa portrays a Persian palace guard.

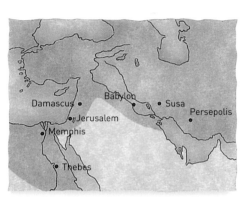

The Achaemenid empire
The Persian empire (shaded in red) was at its maximum extent during the reign of Darius I (522–486 BCE).

Royal center
The great palace at Persepolis was built by Darius I and his successor Xerxes (486–465 BCE). It is shown above in an imaginative 19th-century reconstruction.

Goat
This silver goat (below) is said to come from Persepolis and dates to the 5th century BCE.

Cuneiform (wedge-shaped) script

52

Ahuramazda, the chief Persian god

Lion at bay
A royal lion hunt is portrayed on this cylinder seal (above). The inscription reads "Darius the Great King."

Finery from afar
The Persian kings employed artists and craftsmen of many nationalities. The golden figures on this silver bowl (right) show a winged lion with the head of the Egyptian dwarf god Bes.

Spout to take wick

Sun lamp
This bronze lamp (left) from Lachish was found in the "Solar shrine," a small temple associated with Sun worship.

An imaginative reconstruction of a ceremony that might have taken place at Persepolis.

Cyrus cylinder
The text on this clay cylinder (above) reveals how Cyrus allowed people in captivity in Babylon to return to their homelands.

Greeks and Romans

In 333 BCE, the Persian empire fell into the hands of the Macedonian ruler Alexander the Great. After his death, Palestine was ruled by Ptolemy and his descendants, and then passed to the Seleucids of Syria. In 168 BCE, the Seleucid king Antiochus IV looted the Temple in Jerusalem and banned Jewish religious practices. The Jews rebelled and defeated the Seleucids in a series of military campaigns. Between 142–63 BCE, Judah enjoyed a period of independence until civil war broke out. In 63 BCE, the Roman general Pompey entered Jerusalem. The area, now called Judea, was given semi-independence in 40 BCE when the Romans appointed Herod king. Herod's son, Archelaus, was dismissed by Rome in 6 CE, leaving Judea as a Roman province ruled by officials called procurators.

Time of change
During the rule of Alexander the Great (above), Palestine underwent great change. Long-standing traditions were overturned in the process of "Hellenism," the introduction of Greek culture and religion.

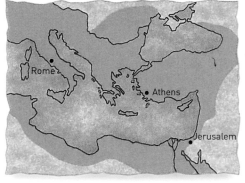

The Roman empire
By the time of Titus (79–81 CE), the entire Mediterranean area was under Roman rule.

From Greece to Egypt
When Alexander died, his empire was fought over by his generals. Ptolemy I, a Macedonian, seized Palestine and Egypt, and founded a dynasty that ruled from a new capital, Alexandria, in Egypt. The Ptolemies were Greek, but were often portrayed as traditional Egyptian rulers. This limestone stela (above) shows Ptolemy II, who succeeded his father in 283 BCE.

This miniature bronze altar of the Roman period comes from Byblos, once an important Phoenician city and port.

Sacrifice to the gods
The enforced worship of pagan Greek and Roman gods was deeply resented by the Jews.

Jewish revolts

In 66 CE, a Jewish revolt against Roman rule, led by high-ranking priests and pharisees, broke out in Palestine. The revolt was put down by the emperor Vespasian, together with his son Titus, who, in 70 CE, captured Jerusalem and destroyed the Temple. A second revolt, in 132 CE, was crushed by the emperor Hadrian.

Marble bust of the Roman emperor Tiberius.

Arch of Titus

The Roman victory in the first Jewish war was commemorated on a magnificent arch in Rome (right). It was erected by the emperor Domitian in memory of his brother Titus.

Calvary

After 6 CE, Judea became a Roman province. It was under the fifth procurator, Pontius Pilate, that Jesus Christ was crucified.

Crucifixion

This illustration shows how Jesus might have been crucified.

This amusing Roman pitcher from Jerusalem dates to the 2nd century CE.

New gods for old

The Greeks and Romans introduced their own gods. In Phoenicia, where Canaanite religion had persisted until the coming of Alexander, most of these could be related to the old gods. The Greek goddess Aphrodite (left) was identified with the Canaanite goddess Astarte (see pp. 24–25).

Roman burials

The Romans wrapped their dead in linen and placed the body on a shelf inside a tomb. Later, the bones would be placed in a stone box called an ossuary, like the one above.

King Herod

Herod was the son of Antipater, adviser to John Hyrcanus II, the last ruler of the Hasmonaean dynasty of Judah. During the conflict between Roman generals Mark Antony and Augustus, Herod played a shrewd political game. He changed his support from Mark Antony to the victorious Augustus at just the right time. The Romans rewarded Herod's loyalty by making him king of Judea in 40 BCE.

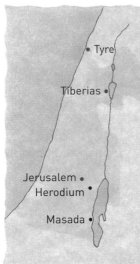

Herod's world
At its peak, Herod's kingdom included most of Palestine, parts of Syria, and large areas east of the Jordan River.

Eastern tower

Encircling corridor on several levels

Underground passage and steps leading from base of hill to entrance chamber

Eastern half of palace area occupied by garden enclosed by columns

Head on a plate

John the Baptist, whose head was brought to Salome, was held at Herod's fortress at Machaerus.

Well appointed

This fine bathhouse stood at the north side of the palace at Herodium. It was richly decorated with mosaic floors and frescoes.

Herodium

Herod was a great builder. His hilltop fortress of Herodium (right and below), 8 miles (12 km) south of Jerusalem, contained a luxurious palace. It was also thought to be Herod's burial place. The picture (right) shows an aerial view of the site today; the model (below) is a reconstruction of what it might have looked like in Herod's time.

Wall of tears

The wailing wall at Jerusalem is part of the sanctuary that contained Herod's Temple.

Semicircular tower, mostly covered by the artificial hill

Massacre

According to the New Testament, Herod ordered the mass slaughter of children in an attempt to kill Jesus of Nazareth. In reality, the story is a myth.

Upper part of hill is an artificial rampart encasing the lower parts of the fortress

Masada

The fortress of Masada (above) became famous during the first Jewish revolt (66 CE). Herod added a luxurious palace built on three natural rock terraces.

The Bible as evidence

The Bible is a collection of 63 individual books, divided into two main parts, the Old and New Testaments. For archeologists working in the Holy Land, the Bible is a major source. But, like many ancient texts, it must be used critically. Many of the Old Testament books are edited compilations, put into their final form long after the events they describe.

Dead Sea Scrolls

In 1947, a goatherd found ancient Hebrew manuscripts (now called the Dead Sea Scrolls) in a cave at Qumran. They had been stored in pottery jars like this one (left). Although incomplete, the scrolls must originally have included all the books of the Old Testament.

One of the Dead Sea Scrolls contains the text of the book of Habakkuk with a verse-by-verse commentary.

The 4th-century CE Codex Sinaiticus, written in Greek, was found at St. Catherine's monastery (right).

Hiding place of the Scrolls

The Scrolls were hidden in desert caves during the first Jewish revolt (see p. 55). They probably came from the monastery of a religious group of Jews called the Essenes.

Turin Shroud

The Shroud of Turin was believed to be the shroud in which Jesus was wrapped after his death. It bore an extraordinary image said to be that of Christ himself. Modern scientific testing has since shown that it is in fact a medieval fake.

Jesus asking for the children to be brought to him.

Mosaic map

In 1884, a remarkable mosaic was discovered in the Greek Orthodox church in Madaba, Jordan. Dating to the 6th century CE, it shows a map of the Holy Land with pictures of towns such as Jerusalem and parts of the Jordan Valley and the Negev.

This page of St. Luke's Gospel is from a 5th-century CE text.

Illuminated manuscript

In the Medieval period, highly decorated, or "illuminated," manuscripts of the Bible were made by monks. This example (above) is from a Latin Bible dating to 750 CE.

Before the crucifixion

This image of Christ wearing the crown of thorns (left) is by the 15th-century Flemish painter Quentin Massys (1466–1530).

Continued on next page

Translations

As the Christian church spread, translations of the Bible began to appear in Latin, Egyptian, and Syriac. This manuscript of the New Testament (left) was written in 1216 CE in Syriac.

Text in Syriac

Moses

When Moses returned from Mount Sinai, he brought with him stone tablets engraved with the Ten Commandments.

Text in Hebrew

Hebrew scrolls

Hebrew scribes carefully copied out the texts of the Old Testament books on to parchment. These were rolled up and kept in the synagogues, the Jewish places of worship.

Hebrew Bible

This page from a Hebrew Bible (above) shows the story of the Exodus. This is quite a recent Hebrew Bible, but the text has changed very little since the Dead Sea Scrolls were written out almost 2,000 years ago.

Scrolls covered in fine cloth

In the Temple

The young Jesus was once discovered debating with the wise men at the Temple. The episode is shown here in a painting by William Holman Hunt (1827–1910).

The menorah

The Hebrew word "menorah" means a lampstand. In the Old Testament, it refers to the seven-branched candlestick that stood in the Temple of Jerusalem until the Romans removed it in 70 CE. It is shown, with other looted objects, on the arch of Titus (see p. 55).

King David

David was the second king of Israel who went on to write many of the Psalms. He is shown above in a painting by Pietro Perugino.

The printed Bible

Johannes Gutenberg was one of the inventors of printing with movable type in the 15th century. His Bible, which appeared in Latin in 1456, was the first printed edition. Printed texts made the Bible much more accessible.

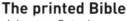

Text in Latin

Text in English

The Bible in English

English translations of the Bible began to appear with John Wycliffe's version in 1384. William Tyndale was the first English translator to tackle the New Testament. His translation appeared in 1526.

An Arab encampment, painted by David Roberts (1796–1864).

Archeology

Modern archeology in the Holy Land began in 1865 with the formation of the Palestine Exploration Fund. The Fund's purpose was to investigate the archeology, geography, geology, and natural history of Palestine. A detailed survey of the area was completed in 1877, and in 1890, the Fund engaged archeologist Flinders Petrie to excavate at Tell el-Hesi.

W. M. F. Petrie
Petrie (above) was already well regarded in Egypt when he was engaged by the Palestine Exploration Fund.

Handpick
A small handpick (left) breaks up the earth cleanly and causes minimal damage to artifacts.

Metal bob hangs vertically

Ranging pole
A ranging pole (above), marked off in red and white 20-in (50-cm) bands, is used to indicate scale in excavation photographs.

Keeping verticals vertical
A plumb line (above left) is used for making vertical sections. A vertical section through a site provides a visual record of the site's history of occupation.

Beth Shan
A tell like Beth Shan (above) is formed over generations by the buildup of layers of debris. Studying the objects in each layer shows how the culture of the people who lived there has changed over the centuries.

Gentle lever
A plasterer's "leaf" (right) is used for lifting fragile objects from the soil.

10m 2 kg BS 4484 0 0.2

General Sir Charles Warren
Warren (above, right) provided the Palestine Exploration Fund with valuable information about the construction of the Dome of the Rock and the platform of Herod's Temple.

Taking measurements
Precision is essential in archeology. Cloth tapes are used to set out the excavation areas and to make accurate plans of excavated features.

Trowels

In the Holy Land, trowels are not used so much for digging, because their scraping action can cause considerable damage. They are used for cleaning away the soil after it has been broken up with a handpick, and for cutting vertical "section" faces through the soil.

Sinai surveyors

In 1868–69, the Palestine Exploration Fund mounted an expedition to southern Sinai in order to examine the possible routes of the Hebrew Exodus.

Charles Wilson

The foundation of the Palestine Exploration Fund was inspired by a survey of Jerusalem taken in 1864 by Sir Charles Wilson (above).

Hold-all

For fieldwork, some sort of site bag is essential for carrying equipment, such as pens, tapes, and string.

Strap fits around waist

Handy rule

Steel tapes are invaluable for drawing and measuring excavated objects.

Bible Lands wonders

Most of the events in the Bible take place in and around the Holy Land, known at different times in history as Canaan, Israel, Judah, and Palestine. Many of the places mentioned in the Bible still exist today.

Nazareth
Jesus spent his early years in Nazareth, a hillside village in southern Galilee in Israel. Seen here is the historic Basilica of the Annunciation, one of the many churches built to commemorate the early life of Jesus.

Bethlehem
Known as the birthplace of Jesus, Bethlehem lies 5 miles (9 km) south of Jerusalem. It was here that David was anointed king of Israel by the prophet Samuel. Today, Bethlehem is a thriving modern city.

Herodium
Built by Herod the Great, Herodium is situated 7.5 miles (12 km) south of Jerusalem. Designed as a summer palace, it is nestled in a hollowed-out hill protected by steep sides. Herod is said to have been buried here in 4 BCE.

Megiddo
This city was the scene of many famous battles, including the Battle of Megiddo in 1479 BCE. Details of the battle are recorded at the Temple of Amun at Karnak, Egypt (above).

Masada
Herod the Great built the fortress of Masada on a flat-topped hill near the Dead Sea. Masada was the last Jewish fortress to fall during the first Jewish revolt against Rome (66–70 CE).

Israel

Tyre

Tyre, in present-day Lebanon, was a Phoenician port, famous for its purple dye. King Hiram of Tyre provided many of the materials for Solomon's Temple in Jerusalem.

Damascus

The ancient city of Damascus in southwest Syria is steeped in biblical history. According to the New Testament, Saul converted to Christianity on the road to Damascus.

Lebanon

Mediterranean Sea

Syria

West Bank

Jordan

Dead Sea

Nestling in the mountains between Israel and Jordan, the Dead Sea is, in fact, a large saltwater lake. Its surface lies 1,400 ft (427 m) below sea level, making its shoreline the lowest patch of dry land on Earth.

Jordan Valley

Stretching from the Sea of Galilee in the north to the Dead Sea in the south, the Jordan Valley is sparsely populated, with vast areas of scrub and thicket.

Jerusalem

Set high in the hills of Judea and protected by valleys on three sides, Jerusalem was the most important city in biblical times. In 1005 BCE, David captured Jerusalem and made it his royal capital. Today, Jerusalem is an important religious center for Jews, Christians, and Muslims.

Timeline

The area known as the Holy Land has a rich and varied history. It was here that people first learned to grow crops and domesticate animals and where the earliest empires were established. The timeline below describes some of the major events, battles, and people featured in this book.

Neolithic stone hand ax

10,000 BCE
Middle Stone Age hunter-gatherers begin to build settlements in the Fertile Crescent.

9000 BCE
Small farming villages begin to appear. Sheep and goats are domesticated in Mesopotamia.

Mesopotamian plow

10,000 BCE	8750 BCE	7500 BCE

Tower of David, Jerusalem

900 BCE
The Phoenicians become a seafaring power in the Mediterranean. Their alphabet comes into usage.

1200 BCE
Iron tools, weapons, and utensils are introduced into Canaan.

1100–1000 BCE
The Israelites and Philistines settle in Canaan.

1000 BCE
David becomes king of the Israelites. He forces the Philistines out of Israel.

1200 BCE	1150 BCE	1100 BCE	1050 BCE	1000 BCE	950 BCE	900 BCE

550 BCE
Cyrus the Great defeats the Medes and founds the Persian empire.

Coin showing Ptolemy I

323 BCE
Alexander the Great dies. Ptolemy I seizes Egypt and Palestine, founding a new dynasty.

928 BCE
Following the death of King Solomon, the kingdom of Israel is divided into two parts: Judah and Israel.

Illustration showing the judgment of Solomon

550 BCE	485 BCE	420 BCE	355 BCE	225 BCE

522 BCE
Darius I becomes king of Persia.

480 BCE
Xerxes, the king of Persia, launches a massive invasion of Greece, but is forced to retreat.

336 BCE
Alexander the Great of Macedon comes to the throne following the death of his father.

Statue of Alexander the Great

Sculpture of Darius I

7000 BCE
Pottery is first made in Mesopotamia. Clay vessels are produced to store and transport food.

Ceramic pottery from Jericho

1595 BCE
The Hittite king Mursilis I destroys the city of Babylon.

4000 BCE
Knowledge of copper-smelting becomes widespread in Mesopotamia.

3000 BCE
The first city-states develop from early farming villages.

1550–1150 BCE
Canaan comes under Egyptian rule in 1550 BCE. Between 1200 and 1150 BCE, the Sea Peoples attack the eastern Mediterranean.

6250 BCE	5000 BCE	3750 BCE	2500 BCE	1250 BCE

814 BCE
The city of Carthage is founded by the Phoenicians.

Gold necklace from Carthage, 7th century BCE

722 BCE
The Assyrians attack Samaria, the capital of Israel.

701 BCE
The Assyrian king, Sennacherib, invades Judah.

Clay seal from Judah

612 BCE
The Assyrian empire collapses.

587 BCE
Nebuchadnezzar II destroys the city of Jerusalem.

850 BCE	800 BCE	750 BCE	700 BCE	650 BCE	600 BCE	550 BCE

Statue of Augustus

63 BCE
Roman general Pompey enters Jerusalem and outrages the Jewish people by entering the Holy of Holies.

Bust of Pompey

33 CE
The Romans crucify Jesus Christ in Jerusalem.

626 BCE
Nabopolassar comes to power, founding the Chaldean dynasty.

74 CE
The Jewish stronghold of Masada falls to the Romans at the end of the first Jewish revolt.

30 BCE	35 CE	100 CE	165 CE

27 BCE
Augustus Caesar (born Octavian) becomes the first Roman emperor.

66 CE
The first Jewish revolt against Roman rule breaks out. It is crushed by the emperor Vespasian.

132 CE
The second Jewish revolt breaks out. It is suppressed in 135 CE by the emperor Hadrian.

Coin of the emperor Hadrian

A to Z of famous people

ABRAHAM One of the founding fathers, or patriarchs, of the Israelite nation. God told Abraham to travel from Ur, in Mesopotamia (present-day Iraq), to Canaan, where he would become "the father of a new nation."

AHAB King of Israel (ruled 874–853 BCE). He allowed his wife Jezebel to introduce the worship of Baal, a pagan god. He was denounced by the prophet Elijah at Mount Carmel.

ALEXANDER THE GREAT King of Macedon (ruled 336–323 BCE) and a talented military leader. He invaded the Persian empire in 334 BCE.

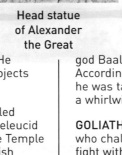

Head statue of Alexander the Great

AMENOPHIS III Egyptian pharaoh (ruled 1390–1352 BCE). He undertook extensive building projects in Egypt and Nubia.

ANTIOCHUS IV King of Syria (ruled 175–164 BCE) and leader of the Seleucid dynasty. In 168 BCE, he looted the Temple in Jerusalem and outlawed Jewish religious practices.

ANTIPATER Father of Herod the Great. He made himself an ally of the Romans and was appointed governor of Judea by Julius Caesar in 47 BCE.

ASHURNASIRPAL II King of Assyria (ruled 883–859 BCE). Details of his reign are known from inscriptions and reliefs found at the ruins of his palace at Nimrud.

ASTYAGES King of the Medes (ruled 585–550 BCE). He was deposed by his grandson, Cyrus the Great.

AUGUSTUS The first emperor of Rome (ruled 27 BCE–14 CE). He restored peace in the Roman empire after a long period of civil war.

CYRUS THE GREAT Founder of the Achaemenid empire (ruled 558–530 BCE). In 539 BCE, he captured Babylon, and allowed the Jews held captive in Babylon to return to Judah.

Sculpture of King David

DARIUS I Ruler of the Achaemenid empire and king of Persia (ruled 522–486 BCE). He built a magnificent complex of palaces in the Persian city of Persepolis.

DAVID A young shepherd boy who became famous for killing the Philistine warrior Goliath. He went on to become Israel's greatest king. A talented musician, he is said to have been the author of many psalms.

DOMITIAN Roman emperor (ruled 81–96 CE). A harsh ruler, Domitian was brutal in his persecution of Christians and Jews.

ELIJAH A great prophet who lived during the reign of King Ahab. He attacked the worship of the pagan god Baal among the Israelites. According to the Old Testament, he was taken up to Heaven in a whirlwind.

GOLIATH A Philistine warrior who challenged the Israelites to fight with him. David accepted the challenge and killed the giant with a single stone.

HADRIAN Roman emperor (ruled 117–138 CE). In 132 CE, Hadrian tried to build a Roman temple on a sacred Jewish site. This led to an uprising in which tens of thousands of Jews were killed.

HAMMURABI King of Babylon (ruled 1792–1750 BCE). He made Babylon the chief kingdom of Mesopotamia and was famous for writing the Code of Hammurabi, a collection of Babylonian laws.

HEROD ARCHELAUS Son of Herod the Great and ruler of the Roman province of Judea (4 BCE–6 CE). He was dismissed from power by emperor Augustus because of his unpopularity with the Jews.

HEROD THE GREAT King of Judea (ruled 37–4 BCE). He was the Roman king in Judea at the time of Jesus' birth and was responsible for rebuilding the Temple in Jerusalem.

HEZEKIAH King of Judah (ruled 715–687 BCE). He was defeated by the Assyrian king Sennacherib and forced to pay heavy tribute.

HIRAM King of Tyre (ruled 969–936 BCE). He was an ally of the Israelite kings David and Solomon and supplied Solomon with men and materials for the Temple in Jerusalem.

ISAAC Son of Abraham and the grandfather of the founders of the 12 tribes of Israel.

JACOB Son of Isaac and Rebekah. He was the father of 12 sons who became the founders of the 12 tribes of Israel.

Isaac and Rebekah with their twin sons Jacob and Esau

JEHU King of Israel (ruled 842–815 BCE). He murdered Jezebel, the wicked wife of King Ahab, and was famous for his fast chariot driving.

JESUS The central figure of Christianity. Born in Bethlehem to Mary and Joseph, Jesus devoted his later years to preaching, with the help of his followers, known as the 12 Apostles. Resented by the Jewish authorities, he was crucified on the orders of Pontius Pilate.

JOHN HYRCANUS II High priest of Judea (76–40 BCE) and the last ruler of the Hasmonaean dynasty in Judea. He was executed in Jerusalem by Herod the Great.

JOHN THE BAPTIST A holy man and prophet who preached on the banks of the River Jordan, calling upon people to repent. John was beheaded by Herod Antipas at the request of his stepdaughter Salome.

JOSEPH Son of Jacob and his wife Rachel, and founder of one of the tribes of Israel. As a boy he was sold into slavery in Egypt, but later rose to a position of power.

JULIUS CAESAR (100–44 BCE) A talented Roman general who made himself ruler of Rome. He was assassinated by a group of leading senators in 44 BCE.

MARK ANTONY (83–30 BCE) A Roman general and statesman who fell in love with Cleopatra, the queen of Egypt. In 30 BCE, Mark Antony committed suicide, along with Cleopatra.

MERNEPTAH King of Egypt (ruled 1213–1203 BCE) and son of the pharaoh Ramesses II. He successfully defended Egypt from a serious invasion from Libya. His military campaign was commemorated in the Israel Stela.

MOSES He led the Israelites out of slavery in Egypt and received the Law (the Ten Commandments) from God on Mount Sinai.

Statue of Julius Caesar

MURSILIS I King of the Hittites (ruled 1620–1590 BCE). After invading Aleppo in Syria, he went on to destroy the city of Babylon in 1595 BCE.

NABOPOLASSAR King of Babylon (ruled 625–605 BCE) and founder of the Chaldean empire. He defeated the Assyrians and captured their capital Nineveh in 612 BCE.

NEBUCHADNEZZAR II Son of Nabopolassar and the king of Babylon (ruled 605–562 BCE). In 586 BCE, he destroyed the city of Jerusalem and forced its people into exile.

NOAH He was instructed by God to build an ark so that he, his family, and two of each kind of living creature would survive the coming flood.

POMPEY Roman general and statesman (106–48 BCE). He married the daughter of Julius Caesar, but was later defeated by Caesar at Pharsalus. Pompey then fled to Egypt, where he was murdered.

PONTIUS PILATE Roman governor of Judea (26–36 CE). It was under Pilate's rule that Jesus was crucified.

PTOLEMY I Macedonian general who became ruler of Egypt (323–283 BCE) after the death of Alexander the Great. He founded the Ptolemaic dynasty that ruled from a new capital, Alexandria, in Egypt.

PTOLEMY II King of Egypt (ruled 285–246 BCE), who made Alexandria a leading centre of the arts and sciences. Under his reign, the power and culture of Egypt was at its height.

RAMESSES II One of the greatest Egyptian pharaohs (ruled 1279–1213 BCE). After fighting the Hittites in 1274 BCE, Ramesses signed the world's earliest surviving peace treaty.

SAMSON An Israelite hero and enemy of the Philistines. He was tricked by Delilah, a beautiful Philistine woman, into revealing that the secret of his strength was in his long hair.

Mosaic showing Noah and the flood

SAUL Chosen by God to be the first king of Israel. He fought many battles with the Philistines, but fell out of favor with God toward the end of his reign.

SENNACHERIB King of Assyria (ruled 704–681 BCE). He invaded Judah in 701 BCE and went on to besiege Jerusalem, forcing King Hezekiah to accept defeat.

SIMON BAR KOCHBA Leader of the second Jewish revolt against Rome (132–135 CE).

The Judgement of King Solomon

SHALMANESER III King of Assyria (ruled 858–824 BCE). He fought many campaigns in Syria and built a great stone palace in the Assyrian capital of Nimrud.

SOLOMON Son of King David and the third king of Israel. He built the Temple in Jerusalem and was renowned for his great wisdom.

TITUS Roman emperor (ruled 79–81 CE). He fought in Judea with his father Vespasian, and put down the first Jewish revolt. In 70 CE, he captured Jerusalem and destroyed the Temple.

VESPASIAN Roman emperor (ruled 69–79 CE). A wise ruler who restored peace to Rome after a year of chaos. He suppressed the first Jewish revolt against Roman rule in Palestine in 70 CE.

XERXES King of Persia (ruled 486–465 BCE) and son of Darius I. He launched a huge invasion of Greece in 480 BCE, but eventually had to withdraw his troops.

Glossary

ACHAEMENID EMPIRE
An ancient Persian empire founded by Cyrus the Great. At its height, the empire stretched from Egypt and Libya in the west to the Indus River in the east.

AMULET
An ornament thought to ward off evil and protect against diseases.

APHRODITE
The Greek goddess of love, identified with the Phoenician goddess Astarte. (*see also* ASTARTE)

ARCHEOLOGY
The study of history through the discovery and analysis of physical remains—objects, buildings, and records—left behind by people.

ARK OF THE COVENANT
The sacred chest that contained the tablets with the Ten Commandments written on them.

ARTIFACT
A man-made object of historical or cultural importance.

ASSYRIAN EMPIRE
An ancient kingdom east of Palestine that became a powerful empire in the 8th and 7th centuries BCE.

ASTARTE
The Phoenician goddess of love.

BAAL
The Canaanite god of war and the weather. He is often depicted holding a lightning bolt.

BABEL
An ancient city in Mesopotamia, thought to be the same as Babylon. According to the book of Genesis, the people of Babel tried to build a massive tower reaching up to Heaven.

BIREME
An ancient ship with two banks of oars on each side.

Statue of Aphrodite

CARNELIAN
A red, semiprecious gemstone, often used in jewelry.

CATAPULT
A military machine used by the Roman army during siege warfare for hurling stones and darts over enemy walls.

CHALDEA
An ancient region of Babylonia, where King Nabopolassar established his empire.

CHERUBIM
A winged sphinx, with the head of a human and the body of a lion. (*see also* SPHINX)

CITY-STATE
A city which, with its surrounding territory, is also an independent political state.

CORBITA
A Roman merchant ship, with rectangular sails, used for long-distance travel.

DEAD SEA SCROLLS
A set of ancient parchments discovered in a cave at Qumran, next to the Dead Sea. It is thought that these scriptures were written between 250 BCE and 65 CE by members of a Jewish sect called the Essenes.

DYNASTY
A family that retains power for several generations, with a succession of rulers from related families.

EMMER
One of the earliest varieties of cultivated wheat, whose grains were covered by a tough sheath.

EMPEROR
The absolute ruler of an empire. An emperor is a higher rank than king.

EMPIRE
A large area with a group of states or regions that are brought under the rule of a single ruler or authority, usually by conquest. (*see also* EMPEROR)

EXODUS
The departure of the Israelites, under the leadership of Moses, out of slavery in Egypt.

FAIENCE
A glazed ceramic, often used to make jewelry or small statues.

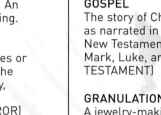

Broad collar made of faience

FERTILE CRESCENT
A crescent-shaped region of fertile land in the Middle East, between Mesopotamia (present-day Iraq) and Egypt.

FORTRESS
A heavily protected building, usually defended by an army.

FRESCO
A technique of painting in which watercolors are applied to wet plaster on a wall or ceiling.

FRIEZE
A deep band of decoration running along the upper part of a wall.

GALILEE
A region in northern Israel where Jesus grew up. The Sea of Galilee is a large freshwater lake and is 13 miles (21 km) long and 8 miles (13 km) wide.

GENESIS
The first book of the Old Testament. (*see also* OLD TESTAMENT)

GLACIS
An artificial slope in front of a palace or fortress, which serves as a defensive barrier.

GOSPEL
The story of Christ's life and teachings as narrated in the first four books of the New Testament attributed to Matthew, Mark, Luke, and John. (*see also* NEW TESTAMENT)

GRANULATION
A jewelry-making technique in which beads of precious metal are used to decorate a surface.

HEBREW
The language of the Hebrew people. It is written from right to left with an alphabet of 22 letters.

HEBREW BIBLE
The collection of sacred Jewish texts. It constitutes a large portion of the Old Testament. (*see also* OLD TESTAMENT)

Menorah and other Jewish artifacts

LAPIS LAZULI
A bright blue, semiprecious stone widely used in jewelry and artifacts.

LEVANT
A former name for the lands on the east coast of the Mediterranean Sea, now occupied by Lebanon, Syria, Israel, and Palestine.

MENORAH
The seven-branched candlestick that stood in the Temple of Jerusalem. Today a nine-branched menorah is used during the Jewish festival of Hannukah.

MIDDLE EAST
The region of western Asia stretching from Turkey in the west to Iran in the east. Egypt is also often included.

MOUNT SINAI
The mountain in Egypt believed to be the place where God gave the Law (Ten Commandments) to Moses.

MURAL
Any piece of artwork applied directly to the surface of a wall. (see also FRESCO)

NEW TESTAMENT
The second half of the Bible containing the life and teaching of Jesus and the development of the early Church.

OBELISK
A stone pillar, often used as a monument in ancient Egypt.

OBSIDIAN
A black, glassy rock formed from solidified volcanic lava. It was used to make tools and for decoration.

OLD TESTAMENT
The first half of the Bible, containing the Law of Moses, the history of the Jewish people, and the writings of the prophets.

OSSUARY
A chest or container, often made of clay, in which human bones were placed.

PAPYRUS
A riverside reed whose stem was used to make paperlike sheets or scrolls.

PATRIARCHS
The founding fathers of the nation of Israel. In the book of Genesis, Abraham, Isaac, and Jacob are known as patriarchs.

PHARAOH
The title given to the rulers of ancient Egypt. The word pharaoh means "great house," a reference to the king's palace.

PLATEAU
A wide, flat area of high land that rises above its surrounding area.

PROCURATOR
A Roman government official in charge of looking after the finances of a province.

PROPHET
A person thought to be chosen by God to deliver God's message to the people.

PROVINCE
A region of the Roman empire outside Italy that was controlled by a Roman official.

RELIEF
A carved or molded sculpture that stands out from its background.

SCARAB
An Egyptian dung beetle, the scarab was linked to the god of the rising Sun.

SEA PEOPLES
A group of peoples, including the Philistines, who invaded many lands around the eastern Mediterranean in the 12th century BCE.

Mask of Tutankhamun, an Egyptian pharaoh

SICKLE
A crescent-shaped tool used for harvesting grain.

SLING
An ancient weapon used to throw an object such as a stone or a clay pellet.

SPHINX
A mythological creature with the body of a lion and a human head.

STELA
An upright stone slab or pillar covered with carvings and used to commemorate special events.

TELL
A large mound marking the site of an ancient settlement. Tells were created by many generations of people living and rebuilding on the same site.

TRIBUTE
A gift of money or treasure offered to powerful rulers by people they rule or have defeated in battle.

HELLENISTIC PERIOD
The period between the death of Alexander the Great in 323 BCE and the establishment of a Roman province in Egypt in 30 BCE.

HIEROGLYPHS
A form of ancient Egyptian writing where pictures are used to build up words.

HITTITES, THE
Members of the ancient people of Anatolia, whose empire flourished in the second millennium BCE.

Hisham's Palace, Jericho

INGOT
A piece of metal that has been cast into a shape that is easy to transport or store.

ISHTAR GATE
The gateway to the city of Babylon built by King Nebuchadnezzar II in about 575 BCE. It was dedicated to the goddess Ishtar.

JERICHO
The world's oldest walled city, first built in about 8000 BCE.

Hebrew Bible

Index

Acknowledgments

Dorling Kindersley would like to thank: Jacquie Gulliver for help with the initial stages of producing the book; Céline Carez, Bernadette Crowley, and Claire Gillard for editorial assistance; Jane Parker for the index; Lisa Bliss, Kevin Lovelock, and John Williams of the British Museum for additional photography; Liz Sephton for design assistance; David Donkin for models; Eugene Fleury and Simon Mumford for illustrating maps; Hazel Beynon for authoring text and relaunch editing; and Peter Akkermans, Rupert L Chapman, Samantha Bolden, Peter Dorrell, Peter Rea, Dianne Rowan, and Kathryn W. Tubb for further assistance.

The publisher would like to thank the following for their kind permission to reproduce their photographs:
(Key: a-above; b-below/bottom; c-center; f-far; l-left; r-right; t-top)

J. C. Allen: 7b, 23cb, 59tr. Ancient Art & Architecture Collection: 43tl, 61tl. Ashmolean Museum, Oxford: 38c. Birmingham Museum and Art Galleries: 60b. Werner Braun: 6b, 27tl, 57cr. Bridgeman Art Library: 50br detail, 57tr detail; / Atkinson Art Gallery, Southport 61b; /Bible Society, London 58cr, 59cl, 60tl, 61cr; /Christies, London 38bl, 61cl; /Gavin Graham Gallery, London 32cl detail; /Guildhall Library 12b, 42c detail; /Musée des Beaux-Arts, Nantes 61tr; / Prado, Madrid 59br; /Private Collection 28tr, 60cl; /Royal Library Stockholm, 59cr; /Victoria & Albert Museum, London 30tr detail. Trustees of the British Museum, London: 8bl, 15tr, 18bl, 19b,

42cr. Dr. P. Dorrell, Institute of Archaeology: 8cr. Egyptian Museum, Cairo: 20c. E. T. Archive, Victoria & Albert Museum: 7tl. Mary Evans Picture Library: 21br, 26tl, 41cr, 44tr. Giraudon Louvre: 41tl. Sonia Halliday Photographs: 6tl, 6cl, 14bl, 43c, 55tc, 62c. Hamburger Kunsthalle: 34br detail, 46tl detail. Robert Harding Picture Library: 10cl, 49br, 52bl, 58cl. Michael Holford: 22–23b, 28tl, 35cl, 38, 41cl, 46–47. Dept. of Antiquities, Israel Museum: front jacket cl, 17t, 24bl, 35bc, 43tr, 58cl. Kobal Collection: 37c. Kunsthistorisches Museum, Vienna: 10–11b. Mansell Collection: 59tl. National Gallery, London: 30br detail, 55cl detail. National Maritime Museum, Haifa: 4041b. Palestine Exploration Fund: 62tl, 62bl, 63tl, 63tr. Zev Radovan: 6cb, 13cl, 15tl, 15cl, 17cr, 27tr, 57c. Scala: 55tl. Jamie Simpson: 12c. Sotheby's, London: 7tr. Amoret Tanner: front jacket tl, back jacket bl, 12tl, 28cb, 29tl, 29bc, 32tl, 33br. Victoria & Albert Museum: 59bl. Zefa: 7c, 50bl. Alamy Images: Hanan Isachar 64cr, The Art Archive 67cl, www.BibleLandPictures.com 67cr;

Corbis: Alfredo Dagli Orti / The Art Archive 67cb, Bruno Morandi 65tr, Egmont Strigl / imageBROKER 23c, Roger Wood 66bl, Sandro Vannini 64bl; Dorling Kindersley: Durham University Oriental Museum 67br, University of Pennsylvania Museum of Archaeology and Anthropology 70bc; Dreamstime.com: Aleksandar Todorovic 64tr, 70-71c, Alon Othnay 66ca, Antonella865 64cl, Arsty 69bl, Chert61 71bl, Ddkg 65tl, Farek 65br, Leonid Spektor 7br, Mark Eaton 66tc, Michal Janošek 71cr, Milosk50 66br, Mohamed Osama 68ca, Mtsyri 68bc, Peeterson 69cb, Steven Frame 7tr, Witr 65ca; Getty Images: Culture Club 66cr, DEA / A. DAGLI ORTI 66cl, EA PICTURE LIBRARY 67tc, Mondadori Portfolio 70tl

All other images © Dorling Kindersley

For further information see: www.dkimages.com